Freedom from Guilt

Finding Release from Your Burdens

Timothy S. Lane

New
Growth
Press
www.newgrowthpress.com

New Growth Press, Greensboro, NC 27429
Copyright © 2008 by Christian Counseling & Educational Foundation. All rights reserved. Published 2008

Cover Design: The DesignWorks Group, Nate Salciccioli and Jeff Miller, www.thedesignworksgroup.com

Typesetting: Robin Black, www.blackbirdcreative.biz

ISBN-10: 1-934885-43-6
ISBN-13: 978-1-934885-43-7

Library of Congress Cataloging-in-Publication Data

Lane, Timothy S., 1961-
  Freedom from guilt: finding release from your burdens /
Timothy S. Lane.
       p. cm.
  Includes bibliographical references and index.
  ISBN 978-1-934885-43-7
  1. Guilt—Religious aspects—Christianity. 2. Forgiveness—
Religious aspects—Christianity. I. Title.
  BT722.L36 2008
  233'.4—dc22

                                      2008011941

Printed in Canada
08 09 10 11 12   5 4 3 2 1

Do you ever feel guilty? Guilt feels terrible. What you did keeps playing and replaying in your mind, and you are filled with regrets and "if onlys." If a lot of people know what you did, your shame and regret increase exponentially. The wider the circle of people who know what happened, the more you suffer.

No one likes to feel guilty. But what exactly is guilt? The dictionary says that guilt is "an awareness of having done wrong or committed a crime, accompanied by feelings of shame and regret" (*Encarta Dictionary*). Since all of us have either done wrong things or failed to do right things, we have all experienced guilt.

You can devise all kinds of ways to try to get rid of your guilty feelings. But your guilt is not just a feeling or a personal problem—it really has to do with your relationship with God. How you deal with your guilt depends on how you view God and what place he has in your life.

How do you handle your guilt? Perhaps you will recognize your typical strategy below. There are many wrong ways to deal with your guilt. The one thing they all have in common is that they don't work. They might make you feel better momentarily, but they won't take away your guilt. The only right way to deal with guilt is by going to God. Only then will you experience true, lasting freedom from guilt.

Wrong Ways to Deal with Guilt

Deny that you are really guilty. One popular way of dealing with guilt is to deny you have done anything wrong. The reasoning goes like this: "I only feel guilty because I am living under standards passed down by an older generation who told me that certain things were right and wrong. To stop feeling guilty, I need to throw off those antiquated standards and live by my own."

According to this way of thinking, if you feel guilty for sleeping with your boyfriend, it's because your mother taught you that premarital sex was wrong. You believe that, if you can convince yourself that premarital sex is not really wrong, your guilty feelings will disappear.

This approach to guilt denies the existence of God (or at least the God of the Bible), and that gets rid of a lot of those pesky, guilt-producing rules in the Bible. But does this really work? What happens when you decide to live by your own standards and you fail to keep even them? You are right back where you started—feeling those terrible guilt feelings and not knowing how to deal with them.

And if your guilt is only a byproduct of the rules your family and culture made up, why do you try so hard to escape your guilt feelings? Think about what you do when you feel guilty. Some people overeat, some exercise, some shop, some drink or do drugs, some sleep too much, some can't sleep at all—the list is endless. Why go to all this trouble for something that doesn't exist?

Try to be a better person. If denying your guilt feelings doesn't work, then you can try another often used method for dealing with guilt: moral self-improvement. You could call this "the new year's resolution approach to guilt." When you notice that you feel guilty, you resolve to stop doing the behavior that is bothering your conscience. Overeaters resolve to diet; couch potatoes resolve to exercise; the disorganized resolve to clean their closets; liars resolve to tell the truth; addicts resolve to stop their addiction; and the list goes on and on. What happens to all those resolutions? Most of us are not able to keep them—and our guilty feelings return.

Compare yourself to others. Sometimes we make it easy for ourselves and decide we don't need to feel guilty as long as we can find someone who is acting worse than we are. We say things like, "I may get angry with my wife and kids, but at least I don't hit them!" or "I may cheat on my taxes, but at least I haven't murdered anyone." We deal with our guilt by being self-righteous and critical of others. And we try to build ourselves up by endlessly discussing the failings of those around us.

But does this really help? Putting someone else down might give us momentary pleasure, but it doesn't get rid of the nagging feeling that we haven't measured up. And if we are reading our Bibles, we know that gossiping is wrong. So talking about other's sins just adds to our burden of guilt.

Become obsessed with your guilt. Many Christians go down this path: "I feel so guilty that I get depressed." or "I failed again; how can I approach God?" Have you ever said or thought something like that? If you are concerned about growing as a Christian, you probably have. This struggle is a sign that God is working in your life. Guilt can be a good thing if it gets you looking for the right cure. If you don't find the right cure, guilt can crush you. David describes the crushing experience of guilt in Psalm 32: "When I kept silent, my bones wasted away through my groaning all day long.

For day and night your hand was heavy upon me; my strength was sapped as in the heat of summer" (Psalm 32:3–4).

The Only Right Way to Deal with Guilt

God says in the Bible that the guilt we feel is real. There is a God who made us and the rest of the world, and he does require us to be perfect (Leviticus 19:2). Sadly, none of us are (Romans 3:23). We have all broken God's two greatest commands: "'Love the Lord your God with all your heart and with all your soul and with all your strength and with all your mind'; and, 'Love your neighbor as yourself'" (Luke 10:27).

If you are struggling with guilt, you are in good company. Guilt is part of the human condition in this broken world. And once you become a Christian, you don't stop sinning, so you need to deal with the guilt that comes from your continuing struggle with sin. This passage from the Bible gives a clear picture of how Jesus has freed us from our guilt:

For the word of God is living and active. Sharper than any double-edged sword, it penetrates even to dividing soul and spirit, joints and marrow; it judges the thoughts and attitudes of the heart. Nothing in all creation is hidden from God's sight. Everything is uncovered and laid bare before the eyes of him to whom we must give account. Therefore, since we have a great high priest who has gone through the heavens, Jesus the Son of God, let us hold firmly to the faith we profess. For we do not have a high priest who is unable to sympathize with our weaknesses, but we have one who has been tempted in every way, just as we are—yet was without sin. Let us then approach the throne of grace with confidence, so that we may receive mercy and find grace to help us in our time of need. (Hebrews 4:12–16)

These verses are both sobering and encouraging. We will give an account one day because we *are* accountable, and there *is* a standard. God is the one before whom we are accountable, and our lives will be compared against his perfect character. This is why we feel guilty, because deep down we know we are guilty. Our guilty feelings and sense of shame come because we have violated God's good and wise commands. What can free us from our guilt?

God himself frees us. He sent his one and only Son, Jesus, to die a terrible and undeserved death for us. Jesus is our Great High Priest who does not offer animals as the Old Testament priests did. He offered himself and became the sacrifice for our sins. The answer to our guilt is found in his life, death, and resurrection. The apostle Paul puts it this way in Romans 8:1: "Therefore, there is now no condemnation for those who are in Christ Jesus." What does "no condemnation" mean for us? Paul gives us the answer in Romans 5:8: "But God demonstrates his own love for us in this: While we were still sinners, Christ died *for* us" (emphasis added). The word "for" in this verse means "in our place." Jesus came and died in our place. He was our substitute. Because he was without sin, he was able to pay the penalty for our sins. His death for us means we can be free from guilt and reconciled to God. Jesus' death is the only real answer to our guilt.

So take heart, and find the liberating cure for guilt in the gospel. The gospel cure begins with remembering, thinking about, and understanding what Christ has done for you on the cross.

Practical Strategies for Change

Freely Confess Your Sins

How do we step into the freedom from guilt that Jesus' death brings? Look at the last sentence in the Hebrews passage. It says we can approach God with confidence. What an amazing statement! Because Jesus has paid for our sins, we can come to God with confidence and confess all our sins. We don't have to be afraid to approach God. We can tell him about every sin and failure without fear because we know he is for us and will forgive us for Jesus' sake. Because God accepts us, we can confess anything to him without fear of condemnation. You can start right now: Freely confess your sins to God. He promises you that there will be no condemnation. You will be forgiven and free.

Learn How to Handle Shame

Guilt is the objective experience of guilt, and shame is the subjective experience of feeling guilty. In our world, we talk mostly about shame (instead of guilt), because most people do not believe that God made the world and rules for the people in his world.

Since guilt is more than a feeling—we are *actually* guilty because we have broken God's loving and wise standards—most of the time when we feel guilty, it's because we *are* guilty. We feel guilty (shame) because we thought, said, or did something that goes against what God wants us to do. Look at how the apostle Paul describes us in Romans 5. It is a comforting passage, but it is also disturbing.

> You see, at just the right time, when we were still powerless, Christ died for the ungodly. Very rarely will anyone die for a righteous man, though for a good man someone might

possibly dare to die. But God demonstrates his own love for us in this: While we were still sinners, Christ died for us. Since we have now been justified by his blood, how much more shall we be saved from God's wrath through him! For if, when we were God's enemies, we were reconciled to him through the death of his Son, how much more, having been reconciled, shall we be saved through his life! (Romans 5:6–10)

According to Paul, we are *weak* and *ungodly.* Then he goes on to call us *sinners* and *enemies!* These are not flattering descriptions. But he is telling us the truth: We are guilty because of our rebellion against God. The essence of sin is to take God's place. Some of us do this openly by saying we don't believe in God. Others of us do it subtly by living a life that does not take the existence of God into account. When we do this, we stand guilty and ashamed before God. We experience shame because of our real guilt. Underneath our anxiety, bitterness, and defensiveness is guilt. That is why we live with the feeling that we are not quite making the grade. We can't get rid of our shame until we address the problem of our real guilt.

These verses point us to the same wonderful cure that is found in Hebrews 4. Jesus takes our place and endures the punishment we deserve, so that our true guilt can be forgiven, and we can be set free. Daily believe in Jesus, daily confess your sins, and daily believe in the forgiveness of sins. As you do this, your real guilt will be taken away, and then your shame will disappear as well.

Go to the Bible for Guidance

It is possible to feel guilty about doing or thinking something that wasn't really wrong. Sometimes it is difficult to know whether your guilt is from a real sin or from your overactive conscience. When this happens, you must have your conscience realigned by God's Word. The Bible will give you a clear understanding of what is right and wrong.

If you read your Bible and are still confused about whether something you did is really a sin, then you should speak to other, wiser Christians who can help you decide whether an attitude, thought, or action is truly sinful.

Keep on Asking for Forgiveness

When you struggle with the same sin again and again, whatever you do, don't stop going to God! Distancing yourself from God is the biggest mistake you can make. All of us have sins we commit many times. If you stop going to God and confessing your sins to him, you will cut yourself off from the only person who can help you. When God enters into a relationship with you, his love is not fickle—his love doesn't change because you are a sinner. Keep going to Jesus with your sins and asking him for the desire and power to change. He will answer that prayer.

As you pray, meditate on these verses: "My dear children, I write this to you so that you will not sin. But if anybody does sin, we have one who speaks to the Father in our defense—Jesus Christ, the Righteous One. He is the atoning sacrifice for our sins, and not only for ours but also for the sins of the whole world" (1 John 2:1–2).

The wonderful truth of the gospel is that you are free to struggle honestly before God because you know he loves you and will not let you go. He loves you so much that he may send hardship into your life to get your attention. This is not punishment, but the loving discipline of your heavenly Father. Please also get help from mature Christians who can pray for you, encourage you, and hold you accountable in your daily battle.

Experience the Peace of God by Faith

When we understand we have *real peace* with God because of what Jesus did for us, then we are able to experience *feeling peaceful* instead of feeling guilty. The apostle Paul says, "Therefore, since we have been justified through faith, we have peace with

God through our Lord Jesus Christ" (Romans 5:1). Notice that our part is only to have faith—to believe in the work that Jesus did on the cross and put all of our hope and trust in him. Instead of dealing with our real guilt by denial, escapism, resolutions, looking down on others, and obsessing, we can confess our sins to Jesus and believe that his death paid the price for our sins.

What are you feeling guilty about right now? Perhaps you said an unkind word to your spouse, your child, or your friend. Perhaps you are struggling with an addiction to alcohol, drugs, sex, or gambling. Perhaps you have a heart full of bitterness and anger towards someone who has wronged you. Are you weary of carrying the burden of your guilt? Whatever it is, tell Jesus about it right now and ask him to forgive you. And now listen to his words to you: "Come to me, all you who are weary and burdened, and I will give you rest. Take my yoke upon you and learn from me, for I am gentle and humble in heart, and you will find rest for your souls" (Matthew 11:28–29). Put all your faith in Jesus' work for you. Only in him will you find rest for your soul.

If you were encouraged by reading this booklet, perhaps you or someone you know would also be blessed from these booklets:

Angry Children: Understanding and Helping Your Child Regain Control, by Michael R. Emlet, M.Div., M.D.

Breaking Pornography Addiction: Strategies for Lasting Change by David Powlison, M.Div., Ph.D.

Controlling Anger: Responding Constructively When Life Goes Wrong by David Powlison, M.Div., Ph.D.

Divorce Recovery: Growing and Healing God's Way by Winston T. Smith, M.Div.

Eating Disorders: The Quest for Thinness by Edward T. Welch, M.Div., Ph.D.

Facing Death with Hope: Living for What Lasts by David Powlison, M.Div., Ph.D.

Family Feuds: How to Respond by Timothy S. Lane, M.Div., D.Min.

Freedom from Addiction: Turning from Your Addictive Behavior by Edward T. Welch, M.Div., Ph.D.

Healing after Abortion: God's Mercy Is for You by David Powlison, M.Div., Ph.D.

Help for Stepfamilies: Avoiding the Pitfalls and Learning to Love by Winston T. Smith, M.Div.

Help for the Caregiver: Facing the Challenges with Understanding and Strength by Michael R. Emlet, M.Div., M.D.

Help! My Spouse Committed Adultery: First Steps for Dealing with Betrayal by Winston T. Smith, M.Div.

Helping Your Adopted Child: Understanding Your Child's Unique Identity by Paul David Tripp, M.Div., D.Min.

Hope for the Depressed: Understanding Depression and Steps to Change by Edward T. Welch, M.Div., Ph.D.

To learn more about CCEF visit our website at www.ccef.org.